Unburial

Unburial

Poems by

Marc Alan Di Martino

Cover design: Shay Culligan
Cover art: Beatriz Crespo
beatrizcrespo.com

ISBN: 978-1-950462-36-0

Kelsay Books Inc.

kelsaybooks.com

502 S 1040 E. A119
American Fork, Utah 84003

for Melissa, and for Lucy

The dead I ghost write
Shed shadows that shine
With hindsight, hearsay—
The last word is mine.
     —Samuel Menashe

Contents

III.
{intermezzo}

IV.
{requiem}

V.
{coda}

I.

{in the beginning}

Runaway

My mother is sitting alone on a park bench in Villa Borghese, eating a sandwich. It isn't an easy thing to find a sandwich in Rome in 1966. She's had to root out the Bar degli Americani on Via Veneto, near the Embassy, in order to find ham on white bread. No mayonnaise. Imagine that: a Jewish girl eating a ham sandwich on a park bench in Rome with no mayo. What is she doing there, so far from home? And where is home, anyway? Her parents' home in Brookline, Massachusetts? That isn't home. Not anymore. She ran away from that home, came to Rome via Paris via San Francisco. Anywhere but at the *shabbos* table with that tyrant her mother and her ineffectual father. A ham sandwich on a park bench is better than that, she says to herself as a dapper man appears, dressed in a smart black suit. She notices...*his teeth.* Naively, she thinks he might be Marcello Mastroianni, her singular destiny to meet a movie star, fall in love, and become his wife. Live happily ever after. The fantasies that run through a young woman's head. This man is not Eddie Fisher. Nice Jewish boy. Dungaree Doll. This man is a smooth-talker. He wants to sell her something. Realizing she is American, he begins speaking in broken schoolboy English. He turns on the charm, and she is charmed. What is he selling? Wine—what else? You are in Italy, poor girl, eating a sandwich, all alone. He overwhelms her, makes her feel like Audrey Hepburn. She, in turn, is an easy target. Not like Italian women. To get into their pants you have to go through their families. He knows. He has two sisters. He's always beating up guys in his neighborhood for putting their hands on them. He's got a reputation. But everyone knows American women are unmoored. Why else do they come here? To get into trouble. To meet a Casanova. To have what they call a 'fling'. (He learned that word in a movie.) Then they go back home and get married to a Rock Hudson or a John Wayne, have two kids and two cars and pursue their dreams of happiness. Europeans have history, Americans have dreams. That seems to him a profound insight. My mother crinkles the cellophane into a ball, rolls it in her palm, brushes the crumbs from her skirt. He looks at her knees, the skin boldly exposed, wonders what's beyond them. She isn't thin, he thinks, as he absorbs her body with his eyes. He isn't subtle. You don't need to be in Rome in 1966. All you need to have is charm, and he has excellent charm. She decides in that moment she will go anywhere with this man. She will do anything he asks. She has nothing to lose, no one waiting for her on the other side of the ocean, no Eddie Fisher. Her brother is married to a German. Her brother the magician, who disappeared into a German woman and never came out. How she would like to disappear into this man, fall into the black hole of him, learn to curse her own parents in his tongue, allow the sensual inflections of Italian to evict the Yiddish gutturals lodged in her throat like fish bones. How she would like to learn to trill her *r*'s, double her consonants, strap a crucifix around her neck for the sheer pleasure of seeing her mother's dumbstruck *punim,* bury her alive with Roman invective *li mortacci tua*—fuck your dead ancestors—tear the crucifix off and flush it down the toilet, having exhausted its usefulness. She smoothes her skirt, a little flushed.

14

II.

{redshift}

Tell me about a complicated man.
—Homer, *Odyssey*

Starman

Divorced, my father bought a telescope.
He wanted me to learn about the loneliness
he carried in his gut like a time bomb,

a suburban loneliness, an unquenchable solitude
born of an inability to feel
at home at home or anywhere else.

His home was in the stars—was that what he
wanted me to know? In my eyes

he was an alien: swarthy, European,
a patchwork of incompatibilities

passed on to me through oblique mutations
I've yet to grasp.
                    We'd point it at the moon
from our small balcony on Greenside Drive
and marvel at its pockmarked surfaces
scanning for life among its lonely faces.

Seeing Red

One eye squinted at the world
he broods for hours at the kitchen table
twitching a restless muscle in his brow.
I am afraid to walk across the room
as his cubic anger multiplies
and day recedes without lunch or dinner.
My stomach howls for him to calm himself.
Like Joshua, he is convinced the sun
will stop for him alone, as he tears down
the last remaining girders of our life.
When I am old enough, I meditate,
I won't come back to him.
                              Just then his hand
in one hushed motion—like wind on water—
sweeps up a pepper shaker wordlessly
and smokes its glass against the farthest wall.

Porcupine Stew

We discovered the porcupine
had a yen for pasta al ragù.
                    —Montale

When we were kids in Rome during the War,
meat was a luxury, though we had more
than most. Our father was *carabinieri.*

Your grandfather, *nonno*—you never met—
worked the night shift patrolling a rich
American's villa. It made ends meet.

One evening he spied a fat porcupine
and trained his flashlight on its spiky hide.
It curled into a bush at *nonno*'s club.

He coaxed it out with tiny bits of bread.
As soon as he caught sight of its ball nose
he cracked open its skull and brought it home.

Nonna prepared it as a Sunday stew.
We ate it—five of us—flesh, bone and sinew.

Double Feature

I'd cry when my father went to the movies
alone. It broke my prickly little heart,
hardened it like bone. Youth blinded me
to pleasures of middle age, how the divorced
scrounge around in their pockets for change
to change the tune, even dance a little.
Divorce was death to me; to him it was
a *trompe l'oeil,* full of tiny illusions
the married can't see: TV dinners, sex
with yourself, Friday night at Denny's
splurging on a drippy ice cream sundae
invisible to all but your own children.

Heaven

The day the brakes failed on my father's car
we should have died. What did I know of life
at eight years-old? It was nineteen-eighty-two

the roads weren't equipped with guardrails yet
and rain drenched the swerve of asphalt
above the reservoir as our tiny

Fiat gripped the curve and my father's foot
fumbled at the pedals. Out of the blue, leaves
lodged in my eyes, and I felt the absurd

thrill of flight—acrobats on a trapeze—
forgetful that we were three mammals trapped
in a moving vehicle crashing through trees.

The patient water lapped the muddy bank
dozens of yards below. Like a tin spaceship
we hit the earth, struck down by sycamores

that caught our car as on a spider's thread
before it plummeted past underbrush
and downward to the waiting reservoir.

My father split the windshield with his boot—
gave three hard kicks and the safety glass thatched
like an eggshell. He sent me scurrying up

to flag down help. From the blasted shoulder
our totaled Fiat was a soda can
crushed by an ogre's foot, tossed carelessly

into the woods, an afterthought. Alone,
I waved down motorists, shrieking and pointing,
convinced I was a ghost until one stopped

while dad disentangled our dog from the wreck
and scrambled up to meet me in the sun.
"We must be dead," I told myself, "and this

is heaven."

A User's Guide to Rocks & Minerals

His bookcase sat on cinder blocks, divorce
stranding him in a succession of one-bedroom
apartments—one had even been a church

in a former life—into which he poured his soul:
his drafting table with its slanted top
and little hidden drawers, his self-help books

with names like *My Way, Your Way* and *The Road
Less Traveled,* his aggregation of rocks
and minerals—this last where he pinned his heart

in the off-hours, when not pursuing stability
which always eluded him. Rocks had weight;
his hand could feel their mass, their gravity.

Philosophers, of course, have tried to disprove
their very existence, as of all things,
but he believed in them. Having no god

the rocks would do. They offered him solace
his turbulent mind displaced and overrun
by cultural attitudes he couldn't own.

*

Raised in the shadow of the Vatican
he had been blessed by a Nazi soldier
who, leaning over his perambulator,

pinched his newborn cheeks, Italian-style.
My grandmother stood by terrified, but smiled
thanking the officer for his kind attention

well-practiced in the art of flattery.
Decades later he would court my mother
a proud American Jewess on the make

in Paris & Rome chasing her own devils
the places of her origins erased
or gentrified: Vilna, Lida—Slavic wastes.

Her parents had escaped the storm in time
to forge their way to Boston, Burlington,
elbowed from Europe by its twitching fear.

She had no interest in lost places, though.
"Polish graveyards," her mother called them. Rome
had airs of permanence, the oldest town

in all the West. It called her and she came.
Ironic, heavyset, impetuous,
my father fell for her. He wanted out—

Australia or America, *è lo stesso.*
My mother's brother had wed a German *frau;*
my grandparents sat *shiva* for their children

so to speak—one married Protestant,
the other Catholic, both of them dogs
gone back to lick the vomit of the past.

*

They met in Villa Borghese on the bench,
the very spot I'd later meet my wife,
then married on the Campidoglio

24

with civil rites. Marcus Aurelius
mounting his great bronze horse administered vows.
My wife and I would marry there as well

with rare attention to tradition's lures.
My father's dream was to leave Italy,
my mother's to be married. Both were, three times

over. *Marriage, American style.* Divorce
was in the air back then: progressive, hip.
Dad took us to see *Kramer vs. Kramer*

when I was eight, thinking it would ease the pain
of separation. I cringed as Dustin Hoffman
trying to cook up French toast for his son

burned his hand on the red-hot frying pan
making a mess of his entrusted role.
The son just looked on in disappointment.

That movie was a mirror for our life.
My father cooked Italian meals, spaghetti
reheated in his mother's iron skillet

till it was black and crisp, drizzled with cheese,
punished me with detested vegetables.
I was the conduit for his angry spells

and I resented it. Every so often, though,
he'd open one of those drawers in his desk
and pull out a tray of vibrant minerals:

round geodes, spiky quartz and silky slate,
mica which turned to powder in my hands
flecked by a billion years of sediment,

weightless pumice, granite, obsidian,
the names alone enough to set me dreaming
of further atmospheres. These fragments he kept

kept secrets of their own, had fallen to Earth
from spacetime, or grew organically
in igneous niches of our planet's skin.

He had collected each stark specimen
himself on outings with old college friends.
He showed me how to use Coca-Cola

to clean the dirt off rocks and polish them
with a scuzzy toothbrush. "Don't drink this,"
he warned as I watched it bubble and fizz

like hydrogen peroxide on a wound.
"Think what this stuff does to your stomach."
I'd look down, terrified, and took the advice.

*

It seems those rocks should be with me today
since he is not. I often think of them,
that he is somehow them, every atom

gone home to roost, bound now to some new thing.
I am not lying when I tell my daughter
he is a star. He's not in heaven,

I explain, but what we call the *cosmos,*
everything that ever was or will be,
a concept which may expand or contract

over time. It is provisional, that's all
we know right now. But she doesn't ask
hard questions yet, just looks up longingly

at the few visible luminous stirrings
above us. *Is that one him?* she asks. *Yes,
and that one and that one and that one, too.*

The Raccoon

He'd empty nearly a gallon of whole milk
each night, metal tubes of anchovy
paste, stewed tomatoes, hamburger
meat he called 'steak tartare', salted &
peppered, black cherry ice cream
meticulously excavated to reveal
a diminishing pink ziggurat
at its center like a frozen heart,
gobs of fruit leeched to his beard
then walk the house in the semi-dark

his open eye a roving periscope.
Once he snacked on an entire tin
of Danish butter cookies, his delicious sin
betrayed by a tower of ruffled papers
on the kitchen counter—as though
a thoughtful raccoon had raided
our garbage while the world slept.

Satanic Panic

That sleek black maple was a talisman.
I'd touch it every morning on my way
to school, its panther leaping out at me
from eagle claw and crystal ball. The stain
of Satan's minions hung about the name
evangelical black magic's long crusade
eroding parents' trust. Our teenage creed
was "Skate or Die"—we didn't give a damn

though evil was the least of our concerns.
On *Donahue,* psychologists explained
to credulous America how stars
inverted like old Beatles' songs upturned
good Christian values, how the dreaded end
drew near, but not why governments start wars.

Summer School

My punishment for falling grades in math
was scouring bathroom tiles with a toothbrush
long afternoons spent gagging on the stuff
I toiled to comprehend, my brain awash
with fractions, decimals and algebra
that never stuck, no matter how I scrubbed.

I'd unclasp in my mind some teenage bra
my vacant fingers thumbs that fondled, rubbed
soft legs of lilac, mane of mustang hair
aloft a pair of female shoulders, bare,
burnished beneath a cloudless summer sky
mutating in my hands like memory

freed from all tedium, calculation, *him*—
sullen gatekeeper—tethered to his whim.

Like Glass

He gave instructions how to polish glass
of windows, mirrors, anything that shined.
"Use crumpled-up old newspapers. Erase
fingerprints, scuff marks, birdshit." His jubilant face
went serious for once. No kidding around.
The neon liquid squirted from its gland
crop-dusting surfaces with bluish foam.
My hands made circles. Round and round they flew,
squeaking and squawking. "*Forza!*" he'd renew
his call-to-arms, eyeing me with the stone
expression of an art critic. At home
we played this game each weekend as I grew
opaque with weariness, just like the sands
—vitreous and brittle—beneath my hands.

Star Tissue

My father, in his final year of life,
          spoke to me of black holes. *Star tissue,*
he read, *makes up the universe. Old wounds*

torn open crafted carousels of stars
          unraveling at lightspeed through spacetime.
(He turned the volume down on his Ravel

adjusting tone to matters of import.)
          A black hole swallows up whole galaxies
until they vanish in a puff of smoke.

It happens very slowly. Each time you look
          upward at night, see constellations fixed
like wallpaper, remember that that light

had left its source some billion years ago
          and what you're seeing when you look at it
is nothing more or less than a past time.

"Even the light reflected in my eyes
          takes time to reach you—infinitesimal,
it's true—but time the same. You do not see

me as I am, but as I was." His face
          was as alive as I had ever seen it
his shirtsleeved arms in motion diagramming

explosions more intense than any nuke
          could dream of. (*Bolero*'s tympanies
burst genteel bombs inside our living room.)

He pressed his book into my palm. Its author
        sat in a wheelchair on the dust cover
peering out awkwardly. My teenage brain

was curious, but clearly unprepared
        to fully grasp what he was telling me.
A thicker tome sat on his reading desk:

Alaska. His world was scientific, cool
        as pure Alaskan snowdrift. I was punk,
hardcore skaterat. But something else was there

between us in these moments, something rare.
        I would reflect on it with longing years
later, after his body had deossified

to carbon dust. Black holes devour their young
        just as the Earth eats hers, each body sucked
clean of its mineral flesh, dismantled

bit by bit to nourish other beings.
        I wondered what had nourished me these aeons
since his departure, his death a black hole

leaving me breathless, atomized, alone.
        The stars have taught me how to conjure him
as he threatened to slip away for good

sieved of his essence. *They hold the secrets.*
        All things come from and return to them.
Star tissue bandages the universe.

Misfit

He'd just signed a lease and married his third wife
when his heart thundered in his shirtless chest
exploded like a field of sunflowers
went supernova. His body buckled
like a marionette and he hadn't reached
the shower before it ruptured. I stayed on
a year with his widow. She patiently scrubbed
Formica countertops, dusted the crystal
dolphins from Venice—a wedding present
from his brother and sisters in Italy—
conversed with his ghost, stayed mostly sober.
I curled deep inside the deafening noise
they'd feared satanic: Public Enemy, Dead
Kennedys, pointed my hair in a devilock,
locked the door. Such was my revenge
on him, on death, on the indifference
of the cosmos and its cold bureaucracy.

What I Think about When I Think about Running

How he dropped his keys in the ceramic dish by the door.
How his teal New Balances reflected the evening sunlight.

How he paced himself leisurely on his walk back home.
How the sweat beaded in droplets on his beard.

How his delicate heart sat heavy in his chest.
How none of us knew the truth about it.

How even his doctors had kept it from us.
How bran was supposed to be a panacea for high cholesterol.

How he'd grill sausages on the patio at midnight.
How it was probably too late, anyway.

How 'god' wasn't in his vocabulary, or ours.
How his handwriting wriggled like expiring insects.

How he thought I belonged to a satanic cult.
How he believed he was an alcoholic because his wife was.

How my stepsister found him at the top of the stairs.
How he hadn't had time to get under the shower.

How by the time I got there he was dead.
How his running shoes shrouded his stiffening feet.

Winter

The night was like a fine and brittle clock.
My moonswept vision ticked from star to star
scanning the monstrous heavens—riven, charred—
for signs of life. All was its opposite,
a hell of insensate constellations
dark gaseous altars on the kelp-black sky

no heartbeat but our car's soft engine
purring along the noiseless country roads.

The lemon sun surprised us with absurd
laughter of light; we crept onto campus
a ragged party on the brink of sleep.
You ran to me. I ran to you. We cried,
neither fully believing the other's tears
until the broken silence spoke: "He died."

We're haunted by the winter of his years.

Timonium

You'd joke it was an element, like boron,
titanium, magnesium or neon.
It must have been the name, the *-ium*
suffix, or was it because as a chemical
engineer your brain was wired for such things?
I grew up believing it. That you would die
in Timonium, be buried in its mud
before you'd reached the taut age of Shakespeare
was what Euripides called *tragedy*.

It was your tragedy to die alone
at the top of a stairwell in a home
you'd barely lived in for a year, leaving a wife
unstable as radium and two electrons
from another nucleus. Timonium
has a short half-life, decays exactly
forty-eight years from the time of birth,
give or take a weekend or two. Our tragedy
was to try to get on with our lives
                                    as if

nothing had happened, to go back to school
in Timonium and field questions like
Why were you gone for so long? Were you sick?
Lucky you, you didn't have any homework!

"Sorry, dude, that sucks" graced a Hallmark card
signed by every student in chemistry class
placed on my desk by an anonymous hand.
In school no one teaches you what to say

to people like me. We just go on pretending
we're studying, memorizing elements
one by one: *promethium, europium...*

Granite

Some families are made of little stones
set patiently on the graves of loved ones.
Ours is of this kind, an uncommon ore
fired in the gaudy belly of the earth:
sedimentary, silent. I take this rock,
place it beside faded hothouse flowers
obscuring date-of-birth and date-of-death.
A spider threads a mansion for itself
in the desiccated shade of a rosebush
scuttling to safety as I scatter petals
revealing the sober headstone. Granite
had always been your favorite to collect
due to its commonness, its sturdiness.
                    Now, you lie under it.

The Hole

The hole keeps growing larger every year.
Its edges gird my world. It eats the light.
Peripheral vision has become a gauze
of half-remembered lore, a loose handful
of objects. Photographs. An expired passport.
A winter coat my mother stitched from a kit.
A chunk of sandstone crumbling in my palm.

That's it. The rest of him is owned by others
I've lost, too. Only memory persists
bringing him back to me like Anchises,
a ghostly apparition in my arms.
Poetry redraws what time erases
but can it fill these empty spaces?

Conjuror

Sometimes I dream you are still here with me
your bearded visage grinning at some joke

or *scherzo* unleashed like a Roman candle
into the night, intrepid as a stone.

A conjuror, I sit at my glass desk
reinventing you word by word until

my fingers feel the thread begin to snap
and slip away. One dream recurs

with striking regularity. You phone
inviting me to dinner at your home.

On arrival, the scene appears normal
as if we'd never parted, though I'm older

and the feeling is awkward. I inquire
where you've been, why haven't I heard

from you in so long? You always reply
you've been here the whole time. But where was I?

You're joviality seems a touch unnatural
considering you've been dead most of my life.

The dream is always severed at this point
just when I fall for its mythmaking, sold

on a reality I'll have to reckon with
the rest of my days. When I awake

you're gone again, your address fictitious,
the faces in the dream long since dissolved.

Redshift

The farther you get, the faster you walk away.
Astronomers call this 'red shifting', the way
    light shifts blue-to-red as galaxies fly astray
    at quicksilver speed across the soundless void—

    In the beginning—the story goes—*matter was crammed together in one inconceivably dense point of light the size of a pinprick, cradling everything in the burgeoning universe. It blew apart, spewing its children forth like froth to populate a space which was itself not yet space but forming into its own shapeless nothingness—*

                    whose adolescence
                    is sacred to us—

Dots drawn on the surface of a balloon expand
    outward
              as it fills with helium, separating along its
        sticky latex skin exponentially
equidistant from each other as medieval hill towns.

We, too, in the course of our brief lives and deaths
             are prisoners of location. We wear its ball
       and chain,

bound to it as velocity increases   year by year   leaving us

castaways, custodians of thin holograms
captured by shaky, obsolete technologies
       dimming with alarming frequency. I've tried

to isolate your falling star

racing across a field, heart revving with joy, an eternal child
                  grasping a mason jar, its lid

                                      screwed on tight

but found it was only a firefly
                      vanishing
                      in the underbrush

hot tail flickering, fading
                      irretrievably
                      into the aggregating night.

Unburial

I learned your language to unbury you
to feel again your mossy Roman beard
beneath my fingers, to be thunderstruck

again by your accent. You were *straniero,*
never *americano,* held on to your green card
like any immigrant with an ounce of hope.

Phone calls were costly then, AT&T
selling you a can and string to unspool
across the Atlantic Ocean. Once a month

you'd dial up your sisters in *sammpietro,*
vernacular for the neighborhood in Rome
where you grew up, a stone's throw

from Michelangelo's copper *cuppolone.*
It was still *Oltretevere* back then,
'beyond the Tiber,' now prime real estate,

streets clogged like arteries with tourist buses
craning to see the pope play peek-a-boo.
As kids we'd boomerang indifferently

beneath the saint-studded cornice, feed
the horses stalled on sizzling cobblestones
black as iron ore, leapfrog the piazza

shaped like a keyhole, chase fattened pigeons
around the Egyptian obelisk as fountains
exploded at twilight. We'd snack *supplì*

at kiosks, mozzarella chewing gum
hanging from our lips, slurp *grattachecca*—
a Roman snowball—mint and tamarind

our favorite flavors when the weather got hot.
You told us tales of how as a young man
you'd leap from the Ponte Sant'Angelo

into that ancient Roman waterway
which ferried Cleopatra to her lovers,
& under whose silt history lies still.

You'd navigate us through your marble world
of alleyways and statuary, halting
every fifty yards to chitchat. *Chiacchierare*.

We'd lick our ice cream cones and roll our eyes
as you talked politics or *calcio* with men
you'd never met. It seemed you knew everyone

everywhere you went, possessed passports
permitting you to redraw boundaries
of circumspection. (I am not gifted

that way. Smalltalk is work for me. *Pace*.)
You'd treat us to a poisoned apple—
mela stregata—at your favorite haunt

along the river, mural of Snow White
beaming over the travertine countertop.
Castel Sant'Angelo with its eerie cells

marked our home turf. Heirs to history,
our spindly American bodies catalogued
each twist and alcove in Rome's wrenching gut.

The moment we caught sight of the rainstreaked dome
the final stretch was on us. We'd walk fast
weaving Bernini's dreaming columns, lost

inside temporal power's broken skull
until we reached familiar ochre walls.
Five flights up, our aunts prepared a feast,

the television blasting evening news,
staccato jargon to our ears, the first
and only time we were a family—

extended, patriarchal, skin-on-bone.
Already you'd sown the seeds of divorce
but wouldn't reveal it for another year.

Your cock—that well-fed American bird—
was busy in another henhouse. Rome
wouldn't have punished you as haphazardly

as our mother did when she threw you out.
After all, a man must take a lover
to keep his marriage happy—wasn't that

the pragmatic guiding philosophy
of your continental friends? Marriage
was not for you, not for either of you,

although you'd both repeat the misadventure
until it murdered you. Having finally set
foot, like an explorer, on stable ground

heart attack shifted the tectonic plates
of our lives, sealed your misdirected fate
senza cerimonie, as you would say.

The coroner pronounced you DOA.
The funeral was scheduled for a Friday
in February, the earth rock hard outside

the stony chapel. The pastor said his piece,
he who had only known you for a year.
We sealed you in the mineral earth you loved.

III.

{intermezzo}

The Skaters

and years—so many years
       —Virgil, *Aeneid*

The dragonflies of summer have all vanished.
    Now people warm their hands above strange fires
blazing from big green oil drums. There are holes

in the sides. I wonder what made them there.
    Neighbors, mostly. Girls lacing up their skates
in packs. The smoke and spark of firesticks

jutting out over the lip, burning, burning.
    My parents are somewhere, walking on water
together. My sister is here, her hand in mine

steadying me. Off to the right is where
    the man with the Firebird lives, the one
who followed me, in those apartments over

there. *Don't go there by yourself.* Repeat. *Don't
    go...*when my father hoists me and we're off!

IV.

{requiem}

...History is unforgiven.
—Delmore Schwartz

Stolen Borders

To be from a place. To never again have to answer the question
where are you from? with another question *what is that supposed*

to mean? To have parents and grandparents also from a place. To
consult a map and not have to think *where is it I'm from again?*

where was I born where did I grow up where was I schooled where
did I run off to in flight from my father's ghost? To have roots,

shoots, seeds and leaves like an ordinary plant or tree, irrevocably
stuck in the earth, an identifiable place of origin, marked & labeled

like any wine or olive oil, a pedigree, a race like a dog or horse—
even farm animals can trace their origins—and not have half my

ancestors vanish like a white rabbit in the midst of the twentieth
century. I've witnessed the top-hat, turned it upside down, seen its

contents tumble terribly to the ground, saw it held only clots of
hair rotted teeth gold fillings adroitly melted out & reconstituted

as Swiss bank accounts. Fugitive diamonds alone have been
vouchsafed across the stolen borders of my life.

The Town Rabbi Writes to the Bishop of Lida

History has no messiah,
no savior—it passes

like bathwater down a drain
cleansing an old woman's body

her skin mottled and scarred
as a fallen fig.

Before long
a horse or child

will crush it to the ground
grinding its pulp

back into the hard earth
that bore it.

On My Great-Grandfather's 131st Birthday

with apologies to Irving Feldman

Who was this man? I've never even seen a photo.
Somewhere in Poland, what is now Belarus
he likely lived surrounded by mud and cows.
My imagination pits him against the rabbi—
a staunch anti-conformist, a freethinker—
but history informs me that he laid *tefillin*
three times a day, said his evening *Sh'ma*
and went to bed with a tightening stomach.

My great-grandmother begged him for sex
on Friday nights, groping beneath the sheets
in the noiseless dark, as *cholent* slowly burned.
I want her to have been a strong woman
for her time, but again the books inform me
she put hope in her children and the *Nayer Velt.*

How would they recognize me, the handiwork
of two generations of Americans,
their great-grandson? And how would I know them?
So removed are we from each others' worlds—
yet who can help imagining our meeting?

"Who are you?" my *elter-zeyde* interrogates.
"The son of your only granddaughter,
Hannah-Basha." "Why have you shaved your beard?"
"Aren't there more pressing questions you might ask?
For instance, what are my beliefs about God,
what do I eat for breakfast, in which part of the world
do I live?—inquiries of import and some relevance."
The old man seems unmoved by my arousal
and protests with a heavy finger, *"Apikoros!"*
Yiddish for heathen, Epicurean.

The language he speaks, an Eastern dialect,
spins out of control like a man slipping on ice.
Time and destruction have refracted it
unrecognizably—now neither of us has a key
to the other's world.
                    "Tell me about yourself,"
I prod, moving a step or two closer
toward the egg-yolk yellow pools of his eyes.
"What's to tell?" "I knew that would be your answer."
"A dead man has few words, but no hairs on his tongue."
"You speak in proverbs. Tell me about yourself."
"You know the story of the prophet Nathan?
You are reminding me of him." I want
to scream, *Tell me who you are!* but ask
"What happens when we die? Does God exist?"
knowing there is no answer to my question

at which point my great-grandfather dissolves
in a manic fog of gesticulations
and I to the endless dialogue in my head.

Luftmensch

for Marta

"Isn't there enough to interest you here
on Earth," my wife taunts, "instead of looting
stars and planets in search of yourself?"

She's right. There's quite enough here to keep me
forever bound to this rock of thoughts and dreams—
gravity, for instance, I'm helpless

against it. She's the pragmatic one
between us. *Luftmensch,* she calls me
using a Yiddish expression I taught her

years before we got engaged, meaning *one
whose head is always in the clouds.* Yiddish,
it has been said (by Yiddish philologists

mostly) has an expression for everything
though to my knowledge there's no way to say
one with her feet planted firmly on the ground

as roots were mainly used for making soup
in Ashkenazi Jewish homes, the rest
relegated to books and parables

more readily smuggled across the border
between two kingdoms— along with a few diamonds
in a secret pocket—than a timber house.

Maybe that's why I look up at the stars
because I know my true roots go outward
not downward, like the top half of a tree

reaching toward the elemental sky
the photonic blaze tightening it until
it's taut as a wire. The soul, wrote Amichai,

is like that—an invisible string
running from mouth to heart to anus, sewing you up
like a ragdoll, each of us a conduit

        twixt

earth and sky, a human telescope aching
to rediscover its origins, to pull the string
as tight as possible before it   snaps

Roman Fever

My mother's face a ziggurat of pain
as she stands weeping at the kitchen sink
      her hands immersed in greasy bubbles, suds,

protected by thick green prophylactic gloves
up to her elbows. On the windowsill
      a few ripening peaches catch the sun

as it filters over hedgerow and pine.
Behind her the refrigerator hums
      bars of a melody only she can hear

"The Sound of Silence", maybe, or *West Side
Story*, silver wedding band twined around
      her finger like snakes of Asclepius.

This will be the first of her three marriages
to shatter like a wineglass underfoot.
      She picks herself up after each attempt

to find another man with the acumen
of a career marrier. She can't be single—
      not even for a month, as she squirrels chocolate

under the linens, behind her mother's china,
in places you'd never think to look
      for it. She eats when she's alone

so no one sees, recites a riddle to herself
about trees in the forest. What is the sound
      of a fat woman eating in shame?

Inside the sugared walls of this citadel
she disappears forever. *Let down*
    your hair, O maidels of Jerusalem!

Her love is not like a gazelle but a fox
fucking all the hens in the henhouse.
    You should have found yourself a nice Jewish man

instead of this Casanova—she can hear the voice
crackling down the line as she lies spent
    in a Roman hospital, wooden crucifix

above her head, accusingly. *Murderer!*
it screams. She plugs her ears, turns up
    the volume on the black and white TV.

San Remo is as far as she can see,
my father at her bedside making jokes,
    empty promises. Yet he will follow her

to America where they will marry,
have children, be happy. *Sistemarsi,*
    the Italian verb that means *to settle down*

but is a coat of dreams unto itself.
America will trash them, transform him
    into a divorcé, cloud his itinerant mind

with twelve-step programs, mistresses and death.
It will devour him. But he is young
    in this scene—think Marcello Mastroianni

in *La Dolce Vita:* clean shaven, skinny tie,
brilliantine sleek in his jet-black hair—
      and full of life. *Don't do it!* I can hear

ancestors admonish on both sides. *Nothing good*
can come of it! Which isn't true, of course.
      Nobody sees the movie of their life

until it's over, reels spinning out of control,
the audience deceased. With the lights on
      it's very different in there. *Long story short*

she nearly died in his arms. Her parents flew
Boston-to-Rome on a red-eye, ready
      to sit *shiva* for their no-goodnik *tokhter*

in a hostile land. My father's parents, *nonno*
e nonna, welcomed them with hugs
      and homecooked meals. "How come they can't cook

Italian food in Italy, *for chrissakes?*"
my grandmother *kvetched.* Her cowed husband
      sat by her, mortified. Damage control

was his job. *Nonno e nonna* smiled
imagining American politesse, serving
      cannoli and *arancini* to ungrateful tongues.

They'd die the year we landed on the moon.
I'd never know their generosity
      or taste *nonna's* porcupine stew, only

beef tongue my grandmother prepared on *shabbos,*
briny and hot. I would imagine it
      licking my face as I bit tiny pieces

off, unsevered from the dead animal
it once had served. Many years afterward
      I learned the most disorienting parts

were considered delicacies in the New World.
It's called *tradition.* It's taken me forty years
      to understand the meaning of that word.

Endgame

a photograph, circa 1981

Seven years old, my back already turned
to the cameras, a stack of Wonder Bread
nailed to the tablecloth, my father's fingers
feeling his fork for signs of life. Something
dead and indefinite hangs from its prongs
his lazy eyes locked in a game of chess.
Across the table the queen returns his fire:
a varnished smile. The camera flatters her,
her starring role. My sister tilts her milk,
frothy eyes helplessly afloat in foam
wallpaper the yellow-brownish ochre
of Polaroid family histories.

Who is behind the lens? Whose artistry
groomed my father's beard, brushed my mother's hair
positioned my shoulders to her savvy eye?

A silver samovar reflects the scene
contrasting the burnt-umber mahogany
china cabinet with its little French doors
concealing sweets my mother nibbles at
folded neatly in the decent tablecloths,
stuffed into drawers beneath the candlesticks,
squirreled away like nuts. They fatten her.
Everything between these two comes down to that.
He'll put his feet through doors, his fists through glass,
smash vases, hampers, drive us off a cliff
in search of skin and bone, a Barbie wife.
And when he finds all ninety pounds of her,
this Circe with her whisky breath and spells,
he'll marry the enchantress, broken tooth

for broken tooth, construct a world of hells
until they've tarnished everything in sight
with drunken darkness, nipped away the light.

The checkered tablecloth spreads out our fate.
The king is undone by his queen: stalemate.
The castle crumbles and the bishops rue.
The pawns lose, as they always do.

Powderfinger

I was eleven when my mom's second husband
dropped a loaded .44 Magnum

into my hand. It was heavy metal.
He drove me to a shooting range

taught me to cock the barrel,
pull the trigger. I breathed

and it fired, kicked back hard
as a playground bully. I felt bigger

than I was, though wasn't sure
I liked it much. At home

he pressed his own ammunition
crates of gunpowder stockpiled

beneath my bedroom walls, kept
his .44 at the bottom

of his underwear drawer
unloaded. I never asked him

why he thought he could protect us
if it came to that, but luckily

it never did.

Intolerance

You must love your crooked neighbor
With your crooked heart.
                                    —W.H. Auden

I.

Our family never celebrated Passover
though technically—if you checked the books—
we were Jewish. You couldn't tell by looks

as seldom you can. My mother planted eggs
for us to sniff out painted pastel pinks
soft powder blues and dreamy daffodils

the yard astir with friends and friends of friends
on all fours like Encyclopedia Brown
knee-patches stained with mulch from fresh-cut grass.

An Easter basket was our coveted loot,
artificial turf concealing foil-wrapped treats;
milk-chocolate nuggets, marshmallow-fluff chicks

dyed lemon yellow, clad in sugary shrouds
dissolving on our tongues, a glucose high
that lasted years. My mother was at war

with additives, but here she held her tongue.
My stepdad chuckled, polished his .22,
his basement cubby crammed with tools and ammo,

traditions tensile as the Exodus.
On Sunday we'd drive out to see his folks
in their comfortably egg-white neighborhood.

Baltimore rowhouses. Meemaw and Peepaw
of solid West Virginia mountain stock.
Peepaw sat stiffly in his easy chair

TV awash in shades of golf-course green—
this was before Fox News—his granite mug
unwilling even to acknowledge us,

fingers cradling the remote control
like a crucifix. The women set the table:
boats of larded sweet potatoes, honeyed

ham, roast chicken, dumplings in gravy, grits,
six kinds of pie—a feast fit for a coronary.
Peepaw would make some rude remark, the nubs

of his blue eyes piercing my mother's neck.
He'd been a proud steelworker all his life
which hardened his innate intolerance.

Meemaw would cackle nervously, "Aw, *Paul*."
But she knew better than to speak her mind
if she had one. Even my stepdad cowered

in fear of his father, the piggish old brute
seated before us with his trembling hand
maneuvering a ham hock to his teeth.

He'd had quadruple bypass surgery,
veins and arteries by then jerry-rigged,
a Rube Goldberg comic inside his chest.

II.

Years later we found a VHS cassette
of our in-laws' family reunion
at a national park deep in Appalachia.
Huge plastic bowls of coleslaw, tables set
with plastic plates, and plastic forks and knives,
children playing Cowboys and Indians
with plastic bows and arrows, hamfisting
plastic guns. Two men appear, faces cloaked
by minstrel masks, jiving, fondling their cocks
obscenely in some monkey-nigger shtick,
offscreen a boombox blasting gangsta rap
as kissing cousins howl their crude consent.
Peepaw, a shit-eating grin (as he'd put it)
pinned from ear to ear like a cheap clothesline,
turns to the trembling camcorder and says,
Gimme a shotgun. There the tape went dead.

As teenagers my friends and I would watch
dumbfounded by the hillbilly spectacle
rewinding the tape again and again until
it practically wore out. We'd kid, appalled
by what we took to be a backwoods bunch
of hicks, six-fingered inbreeders, white trash.
How could my mother marry into this,
a clan of moonshiners, as they appeared
in all their ignorance and tarnished pride?

Yet what were we to them but goat-horned Yids
manning the world's banks from secret bunkers
in Tel Aviv or Washington, D.C.?
Their brains strained with inklings of a vision:
a world gone to seed, stripped of privilege,

America with its back against the wall
as hook-nosed villains tumbled through the gates
of paradise, their city on the hill
reduced to *different strokes for different folks*.

Eventually they'd unsettle Baltimore
hightail it to the Blue Ridge of their past
the isolated rural pocket where
they'd go on pretending the world was theirs
with the fluttering salute of plain white folks
attend square dances at the local lodge
stuff hard arteries with cholesterol
until they keeled over from heart failure
and died the way they lived, in ignorant bliss.

Household Goddess

She was all boobs and tan lines, lace panties
done up with tiny bows, her pubic bone
protruding as she struck a vampish pose,
a sobering sign of her mortality.
My adolescent heart fed on the rose
her lips engendered—what those lips might do!—
as fingers licked the swelling in my jeans.
I came without a sound, without a clue.

Her altar was a burnished cedar chest
my mother kept the duvets in. It reeked
of mothballs, disinfectant. I'd replace
the magazine—each perfect stolen breast—
as carefully as if it were a stone
set in a wedding ring—then lie there spent, alone.

My Mother Baked the Zucchini Bread
of Affliction

My mother baked the zucchini bread
of affliction, a war of spices
folded into each sticky mouthful
her love encrusted in cracked walnuts
surprising our teeth. Crumb-dusted hands
tore off chunks the color of Bronze
Age weaponry; like street urchins
we'd stuff ourselves with the opposite
of flatbread—it rose like a sun
at 350° in her state-of-the-art
oven. I'd lick her index finger
after it had dragged the mixing bowl
clean, its white ceramic interior
shimmering with the warm echo
of her Kitchen Aid's calm electric pulse.
I close my eyes and still I taste
her sweet red fingernail sharp against my lips.

Guilt

"Why do you look so guilty," she'd interrogate,
        "if you're not?" The harebrained question raised
        further questions: *Why are you doing this*

to me, your own son? Dreaded guilt was mine
        arching her painted eyebrow one last time
        before a soft smile broke down her charade

and let me in on it. "Just keeping you
        on your toes, *boychikl*." It was her way
        of checking in on me from time to time.

"You always get that guilty *punim* on
        when I ask a question." She had a hundred ways
        to reinforce the concept, neatly Freudian,

of filial guilt. Did I dream of her,
        or did she think I did? Or was it just
        some Jewish-mother thing? Not having priests

to do it for her, she was on her own
        scattering mouse traps to ensnare my soul
        designed to keep my fraught ego in line.

She'd dazzle dinner guests with a frankness
        they'd never heard around their own tables
        nudge conversation to undiscovered shores

discussing the ins-and-outs of anal sex,
        rhapsodizing the virtues of jerking off,
        bragging how our home had no taboos.

My sister, mortified, plotted her escape
        to Blue Ridge country, cows and farmlands crowned
        with smalltown campuses. She'd find true love

and reinvent herself a southern belle.
        Her boyfriends turned bright as pork sausage
        at talk of sodomy, fellatio.

In all our table talk, we never spoke
        of track meets, tailgate parties, junior proms.
        Always the *outré,* perfumed with nonchalance

aristocrats would die for, a gutted Jell-O mold
        in tatters on the table, chunks of fruit
        encased like dragonflies in amber gauze.

We were a kind of low-rent royalty
        I sometimes think, unconscious Jewish pride
        bubbling up from the primordial *borscht*

asserting its haughty gaze on goyish tropes
        as if to say, *We'll make you gentiles pay*
        for three millennia of senseless hate

by reddening your cheeks with bathroom jokes.
        I read once in a psychobiography
        of Hitler what he feared most about Jews

was how they made him feel inferior,
        each *shtick* a proverbial stab in the back.
        He was reported to have said—& I understand

this as a statement of intent—*I will not stop*
    until I squelch the laughter in their throats.
    For such trash talk they led us to the gas.

Nana's Tongue

My nana's specialty was pickled tongue.
If I remember nothing else about her
I'll remember her tongue, the way it lay
on my plate, a reddish-brown slab of meat
thick and briny. If you could serve
and eat a bruise, surely it would be
that color. Its taste still lingers
each time I bite a pickle, decades after
she and my grandfather—who loved his soup
lava-hot—passed on. I was a child then.
My grandmother seemed to do all the speaking
in their home, as her gentle husband sat
silently sipping hot soup from a spoon.
It was as if he'd lost his tongue
or had had it cut out in a second
circumcision—worse than the first
which merely snipped some useless skin
off his penis, this one silenced him,
effectively, for decades. She berated him
like a slave, hot tongue wagging in her mouth
yenta-style. I'd watch his spectacles
like little mirrors reflecting her back
to herself, steel rims glinting off the crystal
chandelier they'd inherited from by-then
gassed relatives. I never once knew
warmth from these people, never once a hug
or a kindness. Just intermittent warfare
waiting to be waged at every turn
each annual visit to their high-rise
in Brookline like a school trip
to the Holocaust Museum.
I can no longer hold my tongue or feign
the solemn devotions of a grandson.

My mother wasted her life hating them
more than she loved herself. Let them lie
in these lines forever like the tongues they bit
off: cold and mute and pickled with spite.

Dark Matter

My uncle was the first to disappear
in a lineage of disappearing acts.
A photo of him at his bar mitzvah

staring darkly at the camera, eyes
hoarding some abominable secret
my mother on the other side of him

seven or eight, her vision razor-sharp
from merciless stropping. The blades of life
spare no one—eventually, each of us

is butchered in one fashion or another
like Isaac on the chopping block. Her face
is stubborn and bullish, her unhappiness

targeted, precise as the crosshairs
on a rifle. She wears a mask of hatred:
for him, herself, her family, her world.

Her expression has a quality of light
about it, of an explosion taken place
a billion or so years outside her body.

Stars have died within her and been reborn
stitching their tissues across the fissures
of her phoenix heart, rising & falling

breaking & being broken without fail
by every man she'd meet. She will conceal
what happened, reveal it only in old age,

leave it for her grown children to decrypt.
What can I do with this burning message?
Read it? Destroy it? Bury it? His name

was Jerry—short for Gerald—Prof. Emeritus
of advanced mathematics at MIT.
That's all we ever knew about him—that,

and this dark matter swirling in our brains
overshadowing his numinous presence,
invisible and tenebrous. Did he have

children, unknown to us as we to them?
My grandparents sit proudly, Star of David
fluttering on the curtain behind them,

my *bubbe-zayde*. Their own parents, too,
grin ceremoniously as their grandson
becomes a man under the Law of Moses.

Was he attracted to mathematics,
I wonder, as a way to abstract pain?
He would eventually disown our clan,

sever himself entirely from us, run
off to Germany to find a wife. The Star
of David could not protect my mother

from who, like David, took what he wanted
when he wanted it. Lovelorn, David sent
Bathsheba's husband Uriah to the front

to kill him off; he then usurped his wife.
In Hebrew, the Star of David is a shield,
magen-David, suggestive of protection,

safety. It offered her no such outpouring.
The only story she ever told of him
was one of brutal, naked violence.

"He got so angry he threw a hairbrush
across the room, aimed it straight at my head.
Back then they had steel bristles, not plastic

like ones today. He was trying to kill me.
It took a chunk out of my bedroom wall."
I grew up with that chunk of wall ingrained

in my skull, the dry weight of it crumbling
grainy as a black and white photograph.
I'd fall asleep wondering what made him

murderous. Was it what she alone knew?
Was it the fear that she would tell someone?
That was seven decades before #metoo—

Who could she tell? Who would've listened to
a girl making up lies about her brother
as he crept across her delicate threshold

into the dark jungle of his manhood?

Unsentimental Journey

I'd Googled him a hundred times to no avail
until I conjured his cold shade into my skiff.
He appeared to me as suddenly: smiling, hale.
I parsed the details: MIT, a German wife,
his age—I added and subtracted years on years.

They matched precisely—my senses keening, ready.
I trained my vision like a scientist or seer.
Two photos—one teenaged, another edging eighty.
Was this the crooked look, the shameful fallen face
biology and chance conferred on me —to wit—

as uncle? Moved by the singular need to trace
an arc of history, to place one further dot
on the spare timeline of my shipwrecked lineage
I tossed in that ocean no pardon could assuage.

Lost Astronaut

A black hole in the shape of Massachusetts
sucks the light of history

through her frail bones and soft, translucent skin
the way she used to breathe cooked flesh
                          off a drumstick

at Thanksgiving dinner. I formed

in her depths as an astronaut, untethered,
orbits the local stars. Suddenly

and without warning I floated away

forever

                  and have been floating ever since.

Candle

for my mother

I need a better way to remember you
that isn't a bleak portrait of a room
inhabited by a woman with your name
but rather her twin sister, the one who came
to visit me in New York, skipping across puddles
on First Avenue, youthful again at sixty. I want
to find that woman again and bring her back
to where you are, to sit her down and say,
"You are my mother and I cherish you
despite what Time has wrought, its ravages,
how memory unspools like a ball of yarn
in the paws of a kitten. I still love
the word 'mother'—a reminder,
a promise, a trigger." Yesterday, you turned
eighty years-old and I wasn't there
to share your cheesecake, light your candle,
help you blow it out. Take these instead
a few straight words that will outlast us both.

Requiem for an Ocean Burial

Memory is what remains of forgetting.
                        —Joachim Sartorius

You wanted a rocky shoreline off the coast of Maine
with barbarous waves, a few small fishing boats,
a lighthouse reaching out across the fog
like a tired hand, waving farewell forever.

What you got was a cramped room in a nursing home
which cost a fortune and drained your bank account,
three drab meals a day, reruns of *Seinfeld,*
bingo on Sunday. You don't even play.

When I think of you now I see my daughter
wheeling you through the East Asian wing
of the Virginia Museum of Fine Arts, pointing
to paintings of cherry blossoms, inviting comment

as you stare at the walls, the delicate pink flowers
on their silk beds confounding you. *How did we get here?*
I wonder—but I know well how you burned
three marriages and plunged headfirst down the stairs

in a gambit for unrequited love. Me,
I'm sick of losing people. My whole life I've been
a tree, my leaves peeling off, standing there
in the storm, waiting it out. You're still alive, of course,

but no telescope on earth is powerful enough
to reach you. Television fills the cracks of your life
the way your children once did, exactly the way
your grandchildren should. But your mind has gone

for a stroll someplace—a better place than this.
You no longer know who the president is
and I envy you that, the involuntary bliss
of your ignorance; you're spared the rituals

of self-immolation the nation endures
in your absence, though you still recall the day
JFK was shot—each stark detail of your day—
while we have *Where were you when you got the results*

and how many weeks did you cry? You'll never know
what it did to us, how it severed us, turned us
into a Civil War family, Union vs. Confederate
contending it out until there was nothing left

to argue over but a fifty-thousand dollar
insurance policy in your name signed *Luv,*
Mom. Heirs to pettiness. Still, I picture you
clipping coupons at the kitchen counter

on Saturday mornings—that was how you took
your mind off things. Your whole life has amounted
to saving cents even as you lost yours. Bare ruined choirs
sing to you now in your blistering senescence.

Here the narrative   breaks
                              down.   All
                                      the king's
                                            men
can't put you back together   again.

The ocean
calls to you, its patient uterus   throbbing
with motherly love   as we arrange your
ashes

to be scattered over the kicking waves.

א

You'll never know that to your final breath
you were my first and every troubled thought.

Well-Wisher

When I let go, let me fall
       freely, as if a hand
had slung my tarnished star
       into a wishing well.

V.

{coda}

To the Horned Moon

How often I meet you here
above the trees and houses
nested in sleep, the edges

of you ringed, luminescent
as a dropped nickel in a pool
of crude oil. Copper-crowned

night, twilit and electric blue,
presiding above the world
unchallenged. What star

measures up to you? None
I know of. They are too far.
You, on the other hand,

so close I could
take you by the horns
wrestle you to Earth or

steer you forever
at ten million miles an hour
straight out of the universe.

Acknowledgments

Thanks to the following journals where some of these poems first appeared:

Verse-Virtual: "A User's Guide to Rocks & Minerals" "To the Horned Moon" "Starman" "Raccoon" "Luftmensch" "Seeing Red" "The Hole" and "Porcupine Stew"

Palette Poetry: "Requiem for an Ocean Burial"

Baltimore Review: "Runaway"

Innisfree Poetry Journal: "The Skaters"

Poetry Salzburg Review: "On My Great-Grandfather's 131st Birthday"

Loch Raven Review: "Heaven"

My gratitude is due to many people who over the years have contributed in ways both large and small to the making of this book. First, my parents Roberto Di Martino and Helyn Levine Di Martino, and their parents Paolo Di Martino, Santina Vella, Simon Levine and Sara Litsky in furnishing the raw materials: the DNA, family stories both real and apocryphal, anecdotes and experiences it has taken me a lifetime to digest. My wife Marta Brachini, for her stoic love in being married to a scribbler of poems. My sister Monica Di Martino Klisz, for being in many cases my first and most invaluable reader. My daughter Melissa Alma and niece Lucy Ellis, for giving me a reason to write these stories down. My uncle Osvaldo Di Martino, who kept his promise and gave me his blessing. My aunts Franca and Rita Di Martino, for loving a difficult nephew. Paola Nicoletti, for her unconditional affection. Bob Barad, for his continuing generosity. Michael Palma, for being a constant source of encouragement. Firestone Feinberg and the community at *Verse-Virtual,* for offering some of these poems a home when no editor would take them. Samuel Menashe, for warning me against poetry. Alexander Booth and Beatriz Crespo, for their creative friendship. Moira Egan and Aaron Poochigian, for agreeing to blurb a first book by an unknown author. Sarah Russell, for insisting I send my manuscript to Karen Kelsay—and Karen, for accepting it. A thousand others whose names would extend beyond the limits of this page. I hope one day to be able to repay each of your kindnesses in some way. The poems in this book are a work of the imagination.

My beloved mother, Helyn Levine Di Martino, passed away while I was preparing this book for publication. Aleha ha-shalom. May she find peace. א

Notes on the Poems

{redshift}: The quote from Homer's *Odyssey* comes from Emily Wilson's translation. "Runaway": *Punim* is Yiddish for 'face.' "Porcupine Stew": The epigraph is from William Arrowsmith's translation. "A User's Guide to Rocks & Minerals": Vilna, the Lithuanian city of Vilnius, known as 'the Jerusalem of Lithuania' before the Shoah, is where my maternal grandfather was born. Lida is presently a town in Belarus; when my maternal grandmother was born there it was in Poland. Sitting *shiva* is a Jewish mourning ritual. "Satanic Panic": Natas Kaupas was a professional skateboarder who came under fire in the late 1980s because his name, written backwards, spells 'Satan'. The Beatles had been accused of seeding Satanic messages into their songs (when played backwards). "Misfit": A *devilock* was a hairstyle popularized by the Misfits, purveyors of a sci-fi/horror brand of punk music in the 1980s. I had most of their cassettes. "Timonium": Timonium is a town in the suburbs of Baltimore, Maryland where my father had his last home. "The Hole": Anchises was the father of Aeneas, hero of the *Aeneid*. "Unburial": *Supplì* and *grattacheccha* are popular Roman street foods. "The Skaters": The epigraph comes from Robert Fitzgerald's translation. "Stolen Borders": The Yiddish expression *ganvenen dem grenetz* means 'steal across the border.' You take what fits in your pockets. "On My Great-Grandfather's 131st Birthday": *Cholent* was a traditional, slow-cooked dish Ashkenazi Jews prepared for the Sabbath. *Tefillin* are ritual phylacteries. The *Sh'ma* is the prayer Jewish males are expected to recite three times a day. *Nayer Velt* is Yiddish for New World. "Luftmensch": Amichai, Yehuda (1924-2000) Israeli poet. "Roman Fever": "Let down your hair…" *Song of Songs*. A *maidel* is a girl, or maiden, in Yiddish. *San Remo* is a televised singing competition popular in Italy, precursor to *American Idol*. *Cannoli* and *arancini* are typical Sicilian delicacies. "Endgame": Circe was a witch-goddess who held Odysseus captive against his will in the *Odyssey*. "Powderfinger": A song by Neil Young. "Intolerance": The title refers to the film by D.W. Griffith. Rube Goldberg was a

comic-strip artist known for his inventive contraptions. Fox News is a television channel popular with conservative white men in the United States. "Guilt": The reference comes from Ron Rosenbaum, *Explaining Hitler*. "Dark Matter": *Bubbe-zayde,* Yiddish for grandma and grandpa. "Requiem for an Ocean Burial": The epigraph is from *Poetry and Time* (trans. Alexander Booth). "Bare ruined choirs…" Shakespeare, *Sonnet 73*.

———

About the Author

Marc Alan Di Martino was born and raised on the East Coast of the United States. He attended Virginia Commonwealth University, where he studied visual arts. After college, he moved to New York City, where he spent eight years working in the city's best used bookshops and collecting vinyl. He moved to Italy in 2003, where he now lives with his family.

His poetry appears in *Rattle, Baltimore Review,* the *New Yorker, Palette Poetry, Valparaiso Poetry Review* and many other places, including the anthologies *What Remains: The Many Ways We Say Goodbye* and *Unsheathed: 24 Contemporary Poets Take Up the Knife*. He has translated the work of Italian poets Giuseppe Gioacchino Belli, Sergio Corazzini and Mario dell'Arco. He can be reached at **marcalandimartino.com**.

www.ingramcontent.com/pod-product-compliance
Lightning Source LLC
Chambersburg PA
CBHW022159080426
42734CB00006B/507